Learning About Reptiles

BY
DEBBIE ROUTH

COPYRIGHT © 2002 Mark Twain Media, Inc.

ISBN 1-58037-192-2

Printing No. CD-1538

Mark Twain Media, Inc., Publishers
Distributed by Carson-Dellosa Publishing Company, Inc.

Table of Contents

Introduction

Welcome to a series of books devoted to the *Chordata* phyla. A **chordate** is an animal that has a spinal cord and **vertebrae** (backbone). Every animal in the animal kingdom can be subdivided into two main groups. The invertebrates (without a backbone) make up 95 percent of all the known animals. The vertebrates (with a backbone) make up only five percent of the animal kingdom. The vertebrates are then subdivided even further into seven classes: the three classes of fish, amphibians, reptiles, birds, and mammals.

This book is devoted to the special group of vertebrates called **reptiles**. People have their own ideas about reptiles. Some of these ideas are false. Have you ever held a snake or a lizard in your hand? Snakes, for example, are not slimy, and most aren't really dangerous. Some reptiles, such as the ancient dinosaurs, fascinate people. The goal of this book is to introduce you to reptiles. Unfortunately, reptiles are often the animals people love to hate.

Reptiles live in various **habitats** (where they live) and are a **diversified** (having different characteristics) class of vertebrates. They are varied in their structures because they must be well suited to their environments; otherwise, they could not survive where they live. Reptiles may be very diversified, but they still have many traits or characteristics in common. Reptiles are **ectothermic** (cold-blooded) vertebrates with dry, scaly skin. The class *reptilia* includes lizards, snakes, turtles, crocodiles, and alligators, as well as the tuatara and the extinct dinosaurs.

Student observers will use many scientific process skills throughout this animal life series. The reinforcement sheets that follow the lessons contain at least one higher-level thinking question. So, student observers, put on those thinking caps and use your process skills to observe, classify, analyze, debate, design, and report. This unit contains a variety of lessons that will help you practice scientific processes as you make exciting discoveries about these "mysterious" creatures called reptiles. They are a part of our living world and so are you.

---

* Teacher Note: Each lesson opens with a manageable amount of text for the student to read. The succeeding pages contain exercises and illustrations that are varied and plentiful. Phonetic spellings and simple definitions for terms are also included to assist the student. The lessons may be used as a complete unit for the entire class or as supplemental material for the reluctant learner. The tone of the book is informal; a dialogue is established between the book and the student.

What Is a Reptile?: *Members, Habitats, and Characteristics*

Kingdom: *Animalia*
  Phylum: *Chordata*
    Subphylum: *Vertebrata*
      Class: *Reptilia* (rep TIL ee uh)

Hello, student observers! Are you ready to learn the facts about an amazing group of animals called reptiles? Reptiles make up a class of vertebrates that are more complex than amphibians. Reptiles are well adapted to life on land. They were the first vertebrates that did not need to live in water for at least part of their lives. The name *reptilia* means "creepers." I wonder where that idea came from?

The world was once full of giant reptiles called dinosaurs. This time period, the Mesozoic Era, was called the age of the dinosaurs. We know they lived and ruled the land during this time because their remains or imprints have been found in rocks. These are called **fossils**. The dinosaurs are all extinct now, but four of the 16 major groups of reptiles have relatives alive today. There are about 6,500 different species of reptiles. They include turtles and tortoises, alligators and crocodiles, lizards and snakes, and a small group called tuataras (too uh TAY ruhs).

Reptiles today can be found on land, in fresh water, in brackish (slightly salty) water, and in seawater. These reptiles may vary in their appearance, but they share a number of important characteristics or features.

Reptile Characteristics

All reptiles are **vertebrates**—they have a bony skeleton that supports and shapes their bodies. Reptiles are **ectothermic** (cold-blooded). Their temperature depends on that of their surroundings. Reptiles cannot tolerate the cold; that's why you see snakes or lizards basking in the sun. One of the major problems faced by land animals is **dehydration** (drying out). As you can see, observers, reptiles have several adaptations to help them overcome this problem.

- Reptiles have dry skin covered with protective scales or plates to keep them from drying out. Their scales are made of a hard material similar to human fingernails.
- Most reptiles have two pairs of short legs with clawed feet; snakes are the exception.
- Reptiles usually lay eggs on land. The eggs have a leathery or hard shell and yolk (food) to feed the embryo. The shelled egg was a big step in vertebrate life. It enabled them to spread throughout the land.
- Reptiles use lungs to breathe oxygen from the air.
- Reptiles have a three- or four-chambered heart.

Name: _____ Date: _____

What Is a Reptile?: *Reinforcement Activity*

To the student observer: What is a reptile? _____

_____

Analyze: If the tuataras are called "living fossils," what do you think this means? _____

_____

I.   Solve the puzzle below:

R __ __ __ __ __ __ __ __   Dinosaurs are ancient _____ of reptiles.

__ e __ __ __ __ __ __ __ __ __   _____ is a major problem for land animals.

__ __ p __ __ __ __ __   _____ are more complex than amphibians.

__ __ __ t __ __ __ __ __ __ __   All reptiles are _____.

__ __ __ __ i __ __   There are 6,500 _____ of reptiles.

__ __ __ __ - __ l __ __ __ __ __   A _____ animal's temperature depends on
                                     its surroundings.

__ __ __ __ __ __ e __ __ __ __   Reptiles are _____ or cold-blooded.

__ __ __ __ __ __ __ s   The "living fossils" are the _____.

II. Complete the following sentences.

1. Reptiles are land animals that lay _____.

2. The embryo developing inside the egg is nourished by the _____.

3. The name *reptilia* means _____.

4. Reptiles use _____ to breathe.

5. _____ evidence proves dinosaurs lived a long time ago.

III. Answer the following questions.

1. What are the four groups of reptiles today?

   a.   _____

   b.   _____

   c.   _____

   d.   _____

2. What are the four main characteristics of reptiles?

   a.   _____

   b.   _____

   c.   _____

   d.   _____

Herpetology: *Crawling Things*

Scientists once thought amphibians and reptiles were closely related, so they classified (grouped) them together. Scientists today realize they look very much alike on the outside, but inside they are very different. Scientists have studied live specimens and dissections of both classes. Because of these studies, we now know amphibians are not reptiles. **Amphibians** have no scales, breathe through their moist skin, and need to return to water to lay their unprotected eggs. They also discovered that amphibians develop differently; they must go through metamorphosis. **Metamorphosis** is a change in development as the young amphibian grows to become an adult. When reptiles hatch, they look exactly like their parents.

Both classes are vertebrates. They are both **ectothermic** (cold-blooded) and must obtain heat from outside sources. They must move to warmer or cooler surroundings as the need arises. Ectothermic animals have an advantage over **endothermic** (warm-blooded) animals because they do not have to maintain a constant body temperature for their survival. This allows reptiles to be able to go long periods of time between meals.

In some cold climates, the reptile adjusts to its surroundings by hibernating. The state of **hibernation** is when an animal's body slows down; the entire body becomes at rest. It will remain in this state and live off body fat until warmer conditions return. In some climates, such as the hot desert, a reptile may find the need to escape the extreme heat and dryness by **estivating**. This is very similar to hibernating except the animal finds a cool spot and slows down all bodily functions until cooler conditions return. A warm-blooded animal's body temperature remains constant no matter what the surrounding temperatures are like. It does not need to hibernate or estivate as a cold-blooded animal does.

Herpetology is a branch of science that deals with both the reptile and the amphibian. The name of this science comes from the Greek word, *herpeton,* which means, "crawling things." Herpetologists study all aspects of reptiles and amphibians. They are very dedicated to the conservation and protection of these animals.

Name: _____ Date: _____

Herpetology: *Reinforcement Activity*

To the student observer: What is *herpetology*? _____

_____

Analyze: Why do modern scientists believe reptiles and amphibians belong in different classes?

_____

_____

Directions: Answer the following questions.

1. Why were amphibians and reptiles originally grouped together? _____

    _____

    _____

2. What are ectothermic animals? _____

    _____

    _____

3. What are endothermic animals? _____

    _____

    _____

4. What advantage does a cold-blooded animal have over a warm-blooded animal?

    _____

    _____

    _____

5. What is hibernation? _____

    _____

    _____

6. What does it mean if an animal estivates? _____

    _____

    _____

7. What is metamorphosis? _____

    _____

    _____

Dinosaurs: *Rulers of the Earth Long, Long Ago*

During the Carboniferous period, the land was covered with swamps and forests. At that time, the most famous reptiles roamed the earth and soon became the most abundant animals. These strange-looking monsters were probably not very intelligent; yet many of them were so big and strong they were able to settle in all parts of the world. How do we know so much about them? We have learned a great deal about them from the fossils **paleontologists** (people who study fossils) have discovered. **Fossils** are hardened remains or imprints of plant or animal life of a previous geologic period. Fossils may form when an organism's remains are preserved, when the remains turn to stone, or when the imprint of the remains or tracks are left in stone.

The word *dinosaur* comes from the Greek words meaning "terrible lizard." Dinosaurs came in all sizes and shapes. A few stood as tall as a building, while others were smaller than a chicken. Most dinosaurs were peaceful plant-eaters. The dinosaurs weren't the only animals on the earth. The dinosaurs coexisted with birds, lizards, and tiny shrew-like mammals.

The dinosaurs are divided into two main groups: the lizard-hipped group and the bird-hipped group. The **lizard-hipped** group contained the largest species. The **herbivore** (plant-eater), the Brontosaurus, and the **carnivore** (meat-eater), the Tyrannosaurus Rex, belonged to this group. The **bird-hipped** group seemed to be primarily herbivores. The Triceratops and the armor-plated Stegosaurus are examples of this group.

The dinosaurs all suddenly died out. Nobody knows for sure why this happened, but scientists have formed some different theories. Most agree that the climate changed and the weather became too cold for dinosaurs to survive. These environmental changes disrupted their food supply. Some believe an **asteroid** (a rock from space) hit the earth so hard that clouds of dust surrounded the planet, blocking out the sun's light. As a result, plant life declined. Some believe it was a slow decline in temperature over time as a result of landmasses drifting north due to the gradual loss of shallow seas. Others believe it was the large amounts of carbon dioxide gas from volcanoes that caused the mass extinction. Because they could eat organisms that depended on decaying plant material, the tiny lizards and mammals were able to survive these conditions. Their survival proves that the surface of the earth did not freeze. Today, since there are no records, there are still many debates over why the mass extinction occurred.

Lizard-hipped

Bird-hipped

6

Name: _____ Date: _____

Dinosaurs: *Reinforcement Activity*

To the student observer: What happened to all the dinosaurs? _____

_____

_____

Analyze: Why didn't all the other animals die out with the dinosaurs? _____

_____

_____

Directions: Answer the following questions.

1. What are paleontologists? _____

    _____

2. What trait did scientists use to divide the dinosaurs into two main groups?

    _____

    _____

3. How does a fossil form? _____

    _____

    _____

    _____

    _____

4. What do most scientists believe caused the dinosaurs to become extinct?

    _____

    _____

    _____

5. Why is it that no one knows what happened to the dinosaurs?

    _____

    _____

    _____

6. What does the word *dinosaur* mean, and from which language does is come?

    _____

    _____

Reptile Reproduction: *"Eggciting" Development*

Reptiles mate to produce more reptiles. Most reptiles lay eggs on land in a nest. Some reptiles, such as the boa constrictor, keep the eggs inside their bodies, and when the babies hatch, they are born alive. Another constrictor, the anaconda, often gives birth to many snakes at one time. Scientists have seen a 6 m (19 ft.) female anaconda give birth to 72 babies.

Reptile eggs may have hard shells like those of chicken eggs or softer, leathery shells. This is a wonderful adaptation for an animal that reproduces on land. Unlike the eggs of most fish and amphibians, eggs of reptiles are fertilized inside the body of the female. After fertilization, the female's body secretes a shell around the egg. The mother then lays the egg in a nest made of plant material or mud. This protects the developing **embryo** (a developing organism) until it is fully-developed and ready to hatch. This type of egg, called an **amniotic egg**, has everything the embryo needs to finish developing. It contains four special kinds of membranes: the amnion, yolk sac, allantois, and chorion. The egg is named for the **amnion** (AM nee un), which surrounds the fluid in which the embryo floats, offering it protection. The **yolk sac** is a membrane that surrounds the yolk, which is the food supply for the embryo. The **allantois** (uh LAN toe is) stores waste produced by the embryo. The **chorion** (KOR ee un) lines the outer shell, enclosing the embryo, all the other membranes, and everything inside the shell. As you can see, this is a benefit for being able to reproduce on land.

The young developing reptile gets oxygen from small **pores** (holes) in the shell. Carbon dioxide is released in the same way. Predators eat many reptile eggs before they can hatch. Mammals, other reptiles, and raptors prey on reptile eggs. The baby reptiles break open the eggs using an **egg tooth**. The egg tooth dries up and falls off shortly after hatching. The young reptile is called a **hatchling**. Most reptiles do not look after their young. The hatchlings are able to care for themselves immediately.

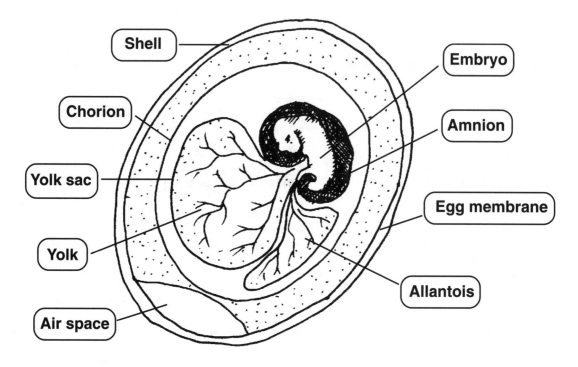

Name: _____ Date: _____

Reptile Reproduction: *Reinforcement Activity*

To the student observer: What are the advantages of the amniotic egg? _____

_____

I.　Answer the following questions.

1.　What is the function of the shelled egg? _____

_____

2.　What is an amniotic egg? _____

_____

_____

3.　 What is the purpose of the yolk? _____

_____

4.　What surrounds the floating embryo? _____

_____

5.　How does oxygen enter the egg? _____

_____

_____

6.　What are young reptiles called? _____

II.　Identify the parts of the reptile egg below.

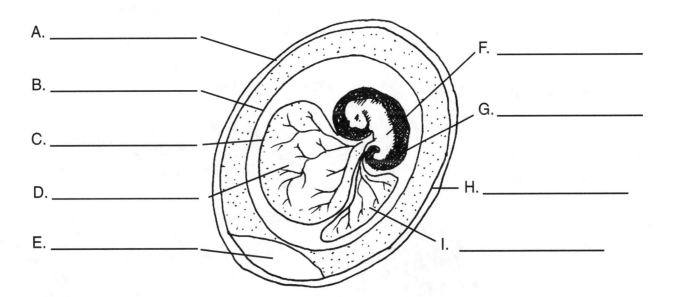

A. _____

B. _____

C. _____

D. _____

E. _____

F. _____

G. _____

H. _____

I. _____

Classification: *Keeping Track of Happy Families*

Reptiles, like all living things, are **classified** (placed into groups), which makes it easier to learn about them. Classification (klas uh fi KAY shun) of animals is based on common ancestors. Animals are classified in the same way that you are related to your brothers and sisters because you share the same parents and in the same way you are related to your cousins because you share the same grandparents. Scientists divide animals into the same family groups according to their common ancestors. Classification is a way of organizing and communicating information about the different kinds of living things, of avoiding mistakes in communication, and giving scientists a logical process to identify newly-discovered organisms.

Scientists have identified over 6,000 species of reptiles. It is difficult to keep track of all the different kinds of **organisms** (living things) that have been discovered so far; each year the list gets longer. In a library, you can find a book quickly because the books have been classified by subject. Grouping things according to their similarities is called **classification**. The science of classification is called **taxonomy** (tacks ON uh mee). Taxonomy is a very complex science because taxonomists do not group organisms together simply because they look alike. They also study their cells, the way they grow and develop, their blood, and their internal structures.

Reptile Groups

Scientists have divided reptiles into four main groups:

- Lizards and snakes make up the largest and most varied order called *Squamata*. The main difference between these kinds of reptiles is that snakes do not have legs.

- Turtles and tortoises belong to the order of reptiles with shells called *Chelonia*. (keh LOH nee uh).

- Crocodiles and alligators belong to the order of *Crocodilia*. They have tails and spend much of their time in water.

- The tuatara is in the smallest order, its own group called *Rhynchocephalia* (ring koh she FAY lee uh). Members of this group still have many of the features of ancient reptiles.

Order: Squamata

Order: Crocodilia

Order: Chelonia

Order: Rhynchocephalia

Name: _____ Date: _____

Classification: *Reinforcement Activity*

To the student observer: Can you explain why classification is necessary? _____

_____

Analyze: Why can't taxonomists group organisms simply by their appearance? _____

_____

_____

Directions: Answer the following questions.

1. What does it mean to "classify" living things? _____

    _____

2. What are two reasons scientists classify organisms? _____

    _____

    _____

    _____

3. What is a taxonomist? _____

    _____

4. What is classification of reptiles based upon? _____

    _____

    _____

5. List the four main orders of reptiles.

    a. _____

    b. _____

    c. _____

    d. _____

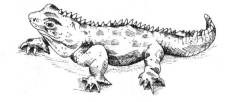

6. List the different characteristics scientists use to classify organisms.

    a. _____

    b. _____

    c. _____

    d. _____

    e. _____

Classification of Modern Reptiles: *Reptile Orders*

Tuataras—The "living fossils"

Class: *Reptilia*

  Order: *Rhynchocephalia* (ring koh she FAY lee uh)

    The **tuataras** (too uh TAY ruhs) are the oldest and smallest order of reptiles. They are in a group of their own. They are sometimes referred to as the "living fossils." The tuatara is a species from New Zealand that resembles a large lizard. They are the last surviving species of primitive reptiles. Their survival is largely due to their remote location, living on isolated islands off the coast of New Zealand. The New Zealand government passed strict laws to protect their isolated homes. However, they are still experiencing some decline in numbers due to the increased population of the Polynesian rats that feed on young tuataras.

    The tuataras eat mostly crickets, seabird eggs, earthworms, and snails. They depend on the seabirds for their existence. In fact, they share their burrows with the seabirds because the seabirds' droppings attract large numbers of their favorite insect snacks. This provides a perfect feeding ground for the tuataras.

Tuataras are scaly and have the tail and face of a lizard. They have spines that run along their backs.

12

Classification of Modern Reptiles: *Reptile Orders (cont.)*

Turtles and Tortoises—Life in a Shell

Class: *Reptilia*
  Order: *Chelonia* (keh LOH nee uh)

Turtles and tortoises are another of the oldest living orders. There are more than 200 species of this order called **Chelonians**. They are divided into three groups: tortoises, sea turtles, and freshwater turtles. They live on every continent except Antarctica.

A Chelonian moves very slowly but is strong and well-protected by its shell. The shell is made up of plates of bone connected at the ribs and backbone. A thin layer of skin covers the shell. The skin is covered with **scutes** (horny scales). Scutes work for the turtle in much the same way that scales work for the snake. Turtles and their shells continue to grow after they become adults. The shell is made up of two parts. The top part is called the **carapace**, and the bottom part is called the **plastron**. The carapace and the plastron are joined together with openings for the turtle's legs, head, and tail. Most turtles can completely retract into their shells. If you could look inside the arched carapace, you would see that a turtle's backbone and ribs are part of the shell; this is why a turtle never comes out of its shell.

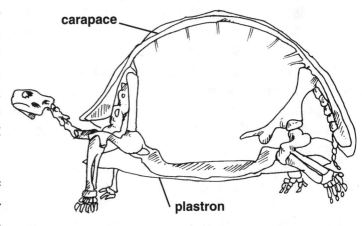

All Chelonians lay eggs on land. Some lay their eggs in sand, some in leaf nests, and some in the burrows of other animals. The number of eggs laid at one time varies with the size of the reptile. Smaller species lay one to four eggs per clutch. Sea turtles, which are the largest members of this group, may lay over 100 eggs at a time.

Similar But Different

Turtles and tortoises look very much alike, but there are important differences. Turtles live in water and have thin, light shells that are flatter to help them swim. A turtle's feet are suited to the type of life it leads. The freshwater turtles have separate toes with claws and often have webbing between their toes. Sea turtles have toes that look like flippers. Tortoises live entirely on land and have thick, strong shells that are dome-shaped. Tortoises have toes that are fused together much like an elephant's toes. Because they are so well-protected from predators, they can live a very long time. The giant tortoise of the Galapagos Islands has been known to live for 150 years. There are several species of Chelonians that are endangered, which is mostly due to the destruction of their habitats.

13

Classification of Modern Reptiles: *Reptile Orders (cont.)*

Crocodiles and Alligators—Large Lizard-like Reptiles

Class: *Reptilia*
   Order: *Crocodilians* (kroc uh DIL ee uns)

The order of **Crocodilians** contains large lizard-like reptiles that include crocodiles, alligators, caimans, and gavials. Crocodilians have sharp teeth, long snouts, heavy bodies, and large muscular tails. Their skin is covered with scutes or scales. They are **nocturnal** (active at night) predators. During the day, they bask in the sun. Crocodilians live together in large groups. They inhabit shallow waters in warm areas of the world. Crocodilians are different from the other members of this class. They have a four-chambered heart and, despite their ferocity, give attentive care to their young. There are 21 species, which are divided into two families.

The first family, **crocodilidae**, is made up of gavials and crocodiles. They usually live in brackish (slightly salty) water. Most of the gavial population live in India. They have long, slender snouts that are suited for catching fish as they sweep through the water. The American Crocodile can be found in the Florida Bay and the Florida Keys; however, its population is on the decline in the United States. Crocodiles are abundant in the tropics of Africa, Asia, Australia, and South America. Crocodiles have long, V-shaped snouts with a large visible tooth on each side. They have eyes, nostrils, and ear openings that are set high on their heads, allowing them to breathe and see while being almost totally submerged in water. **Membranes** (thin layers of skin) close the nostrils, throat, and ears so water cannot get in when the reptile dives. Female crocodiles lay their eggs in a mound of vegetation, cover them up, and leave the nest unguarded.

The second family, the **alligatordae**, is made up of alligators and caimans. Alligators are freshwater reptiles that inhabit swamps, lakes, and rivers. Caimans live in Mexico and throughout South America. Alligators live in the tropics of China and the southern parts of the United States. Both alligators and caimans have short, broad, U-shaped snouts. Their teeth are not visible when the mouth is closed, and they are less aggressive than the crocodiles. Female alligators lay their eggs in huge nests of vegetation, and the females stay to guard their nests.

Alligator or Crocodile?

An alligator has a short, broad, U-shaped snout

A crocodile has a long, narrow V-shaped snout

Classification of Modern Reptiles: *Reptile Orders (cont.)*

Lizards and Snakes—The Largest Group

Class: *Reptilia*

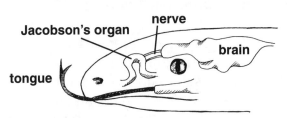

Order: *Squamata*

Snakes and lizards have been very success-ful members of class *reptilia.* Snakes and lizards live on every continent except for the cold polar region of Antarctica. At first, snakes and lizards seem quite different. Snakes are long, legless reptiles that slither along the ground on their bellies. They do not have movable eyelids or external ears. A lizard runs about on all fours and has a tail. They do have movable eyelids and external ears. So how do they fit in the same group?

Scientists have discovered they have many things in common. They both have teeth that grow right out of their jawbones. They both have similar scales. They are always flicking out their tongues, which is how they smell. They both use a special sensory organ called **Jacobson's organ**. As snakes and lizards flick out their tongues, they catch scent particles from the air. By touching their tongues to their Jacobson's organ, they can smell if they are close to food or enemies.

Snakes and lizards fascinate people, and they are sometimes kept as pets. Common pets include boas, garter snakes, corn snakes, chameleons, and iguanas. Snakes and lizards are very clean animals. They are actually helpful because they eat harmful insects and help keep the mice population in check. Snakes and lizards belong to the order *squamata,* which means "scaly" in Latin.

Lizards—Suborder: *Lacertilia*

Lizards are reptiles that have four short legs, a tail, and live mostly on land. There are over 3,000 species of lizards in many shapes and sizes. The prickly gecko is so tiny it's about the size of your thumb. The largest lizard is the Komodo dragon, which can grow to 3 m (10 ft.) long and weigh 166 kg (365 lbs.). Lizards have many specialized adaptations that allow them to live in a wide variety of habitats. Although most live on the ground, many live in burrows, some in trees, and a few even live in water. There are only two species of poisonous lizards; the Gila monster and the Mexican beaded lizard. Lizards are the most successful of all the reptilian groups.

Lizards usually have four short legs and are very quick. Lizards like to eat insects or vegetation. The males are different in color, so they can attract a mate. Some lizards have prehensile tails that they can use to wrap around branches of trees to support their bodies and prevent an unexpected fall. Never grab a lizard by its tail. One defense they have for survival is to break off their tails to escape from predators. Don't worry, the tails **regenerate** (grow back) quickly. Some lizards have special eyes that swivel in all directions. This allows them to continue eating while still watching out for predators. Another adaptation lizards sometimes have is the ability to change their color to blend in with their surroundings. The basilisk can actually use its incredible speed and long, thin toes to walk on water. Others can parachute or fly. Have you ever heard the expression "leaping lizards"?

Classification of Modern Reptiles: *Reptile Orders (cont.)*

Snakes—Suborder: *Surpentes*

Snakes are long reptiles without legs. They are also a very successful group. Snakes live in tunnels and burrows below the ground, above the ground in trees, or in the water. They use their senses to find food and to avoid predators. Some snakes are very colorful or have distinct patterns. Their colors and markings help make identification easy. Most snakes are not poisonous—only 800 out of 2,700 species are venomous. Of those species, only 250 are dangerous to people. Most snakes bite when they feel the need to protect themselves.

The largest snakes in the world are **constrictors**, which squeeze their prey until the animals cannot breathe. The anaconda and the reticulated python can grow up to 9 m (30 ft.) long. Snakes' teeth are well-suited to help them swallow their prey whole. They use their teeth to grab and pull the prey into their gullet. The hinges on a snake's jaws allow it to open its mouth very wide. Some species of snakes can dislocate their jaws to swallow very large prey.

Some snakes use their **venom** (poison) to kill their prey. Venom is produced in glands similar to our saliva glands. All snakes have these glands, but only a small percent produce venom. Snakes that produce their own poison are called **venomous snakes**. The glands pass the venom through a tube into the fang. Snakes have two fangs, one on each side of their upper jaw. The venom enters the prey through a hole in the tip of each fang when the snake bites the victim. Sometimes the venom is so powerful that it kills the prey almost instantly. Other snakes produce a poison that causes a slow and painful death. But remember, only about 250 out of 2,700 produce harmful venom. The most dangerous snakes are the pit vipers: copperheads, cottonmouths (water moccasins), and rattlesnakes. They have sensory organs that can detect the body heat of their prey.

Snakes in motion use one of four methods to move, depending on the shapes of their bodies and their habitats. In **concertina motion**, the snake bunches up its body and then extends forward. Snakes in **rectilinear motion** use muscles to creep along the ground in a fairly straight line. In the **serpentine motion**, the snake moves like a wave against the ground. **Sidewinders** lift their heads and throw their bodies from side to side.

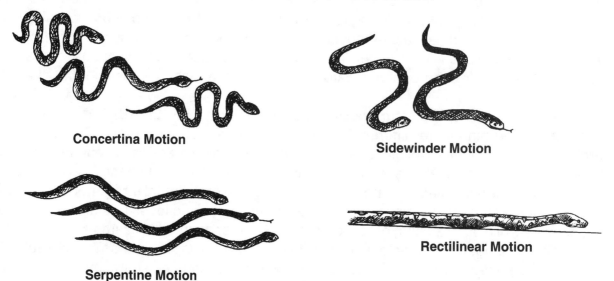

Concertina Motion

Sidewinder Motion

Serpentine Motion

Rectilinear Motion

Name: _____ Date: _____

Classification of Modern Reptiles: *Reinforcement Activity*

To the student observer: Scientists have learned from milking snakes' venom that we can make *antivenin*. Antivenin is a chemical that neutralizes a snake's venom. Until recently, the antivenin has only been useful in treating the venom of a particular species. If you do not know what kind of snake bit you, the physician doesn't know which antivenin to use. The Australian tiger snake preys on other poisonous snakes. It seems to be able to produce an antivenin that neutralizes not only his own venom, but the venom of various other snakes as well.

Analyze: Do you think scientists should be interested in this snake? Why? _____

_____

Directions: Complete the questions below about the different types of modern reptiles.

1. Which order has only a single species? _____

2. What are the main differences between turtles and tortoises? _____

_____

_____

3. Why can't a turtle leave its shell? _____

_____

4. How can you tell the difference between an alligator and a crocodile?

_____

_____

5. Why are the crocodilians different from the other members of class reptilia?

_____

_____

6. How do lizards and snakes find their food since some of them have poor eyesight?

_____

_____

7. How do lizards escape from predators who grab their tails?

_____

_____

8. How do snakes swallow such large prey? _____

_____

_____

Name: _____ Date: _____

Applying Main Ideas: *Which Reptile Is That?*

To the student observer: Identify and describe the main ideas of your reptile unit by completing the following.

1. Identify each of the reptiles below. Then find and circle the reptile names in the word search below.

crocodile   tortoise   alligator   snake   lizard   tuatara   turtle

a. _____

b. _____

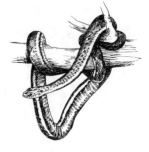

c. _____

d. _____

e. _____

f. _____

g. _____

```
Z A Y K E K A N S V Y W
U I E P M T H K Y J Q T
P A G L D R A Z I L O J
A R J R I D R S Q R F L
G A K O F D N A T Q I J
X T D T Y S O O Y D Y R
U A Z A D E I C B L P R
C U M G G S L D O R R T
F T E I E L X T O R T Z
V V Q L T Z A G R U C V
D W R L C D C A B U X D
L P J A L L U A K C T D
```

18

Name: _____ Date: _____

Reptile Orders: *Reinforcement Activity*

To the student observer: As you have learned, reptiles have many adaptations. There are four remaining groups of modern reptiles and one group of ancient reptiles. See if you can identify the proper examples from each group, using the word bank below. (Two words will not be used.)

triceratops	**tuatara**	**king snake**	**boa**	**iguana**
chameleon	**stegosaurus**	**anaconda**	**terrapin**	**leatherback**
flying dragon	**ridley**	**gopher tortoise**	**skink**	**king cobra**
gavial	**alligator**	**salamander**	**toad**	**cottonmouth**

1. **Order:** *Rhynchocephalia*
   Characteristics: smallest order, have spikes, referred to as "living fossils," live in remote locations
   Examples: _____

   _____

2. **Order:** *Chelonia*
   Characteristics: slow-moving, have scutes and shells
   Examples: _____

   _____

3. **Order:** *Crocodilians*
   Characteristics: two families, give some parental care, have a four-chambered heart, a short, broad, U-shaped snout, and teeth are not visible when mouth is closed
   Examples: _____

   _____

4. **Order:** *Squamata*
   Characteristics: the largest group, some produce venom, have Jacobson's organ, scales, forked-tongue, use camouflage
   Examples: _____

   _____

5. **Order:** *Cotylosaurs*
   Characteristics: Mesozoic era, extinct, studied by paleontologists
   Examples: _____

   _____

Name: _____ Date: _____

Snakes in Your Backyard: *Research and Observation*

To the student observer: Research to identify how many different species of snakes live in your area. Try to discover if there are any poisonous species. If so, be able to identify them. (There are only four poisonous species in the United States.) Where would you be most likely to see the various snakes? Study your snakes, campers!

Directions: Fill in the chart below as you conduct your research.

Snakes in _____ (your state or region)

There are approximately _____ species of snakes.

Snake	Poisonous	Non-poisonous	Where most likely found

Name: _____ Date: _____

Snakes: *Fact or Fiction Reinforcement Activity*

To the student observer: After reading the statements below, determine if the statement is fact or fiction. If the statement is a fact, write "fact" on the line provided; if it is not a fact, write the word "fiction" on the line provided.

_____ 1. Snakes are very clean animals.

_____ 2. Snakes feel slimy when you touch them.

_____ 3. Snakes have keen eyesight.

_____ 4. Snakes use their tongues to help them smell.

_____ 5. Snakes swallow their prey whole.

_____ 6. Snakes do not have teeth.

_____ 7. Snakes live on every continent.

_____ 8. Most snakes lay amniotic eggs.

_____ 9. A snake closes its eyes when it sleeps.

_____ 10. There are only four kinds of poisonous snakes in the United States.

_____ 11. Some snakes molt or shed their skin.

_____ 12. You can milk a snake.

_____ 13. Snakes eat one meal every day, usually in the morning.

_____ 14. A snake can swallow a chicken whole by dislocating its jaw.

_____ 15. All snakes are carnivores.

Reptile Behavior: *Reptiles Do the Strangest Things*

In order to survive, all living things must be able to react well to their surroundings. If they are unable to react well in their surroundings, the picture of survival becomes very bleak. Reptiles have many wonderful adaptations that help them survive in the habitat in which they live. They use their wonderful senses to help them know how to react. For instance, did you know a chameleon is a lizard that can look backward with one eye and forward with the other? They can move each eye independently, and they have a wide field of vision. They use this ability to see all the way around themselves as they move toward their prey. One eye focuses on the prey, while the other keeps watch. Then once they are close enough, the other eye focuses on the prey, and this gives the lizard the ability to shoot its tongue out at lightning speed and grab its victim with deadly accuracy. Vision is just one of the senses animals use to get information about what is going on in the environment. Any change in the environment that is detected by a sense organ is called a **stimulus**. A stimulus is the "something in the environment" that causes the animal to make a **response** or change. The stimulus is the cause of the behavior. Heat, pressure, chemicals, sounds, light, and even gravity are examples of stimuli. Reptiles rely on sight, hearing, smell, and touch just like many other animals do to detect stimuli.

Behavior

Behavior is the way an organism acts. Most behaviors are focused on the need to survive. Behaviors help reptiles avoid predators and find food, water, shelter, and mates. Behaviors can be **inborn** (innate) or **acquired** (learned). Innate behavior is behavior the animal is born knowing how to do. Learned behavior is behavior that is acquired over time as a result of experience. Innate behaviors are reflex acts or instincts. **Reflex acts** are automatic responses in which the brain is not involved. **Instinctive behaviors** require thought processes and are a bit more complex. **Learned behaviors** include conditioning, trial and error, reasoning (insight), and imprinting. Reptiles demonstrate mostly innate forms of behavior. One innate behavior of some reptiles is to molt (shed their skin) in order to grow. Reptiles use sounds, visual displays, and scents as behavior to convey information.

Staying Alive—Defensive Behaviors

Running and Hiding

Most reptiles prefer a quiet day of searching for food, basking in the sun, and avoiding danger. When they are threatened, most reptiles will use the number one method of defense—running and hiding. Even venomous snakes prefer to get out of sight. Many lizards are as fast as lightning and dash away as soon as they sense danger. Some are so quick they can skim across the top of water or sand without sinking. Others glide away by jumping from tree to tree. They extend flaps of skin on their sides that support them in the air. They may fly or glide in the air for up to 9 m (30 ft). Now that's a defensive behavior that is bound to come in handy!

Reptile Behavior: *Reptiles Do the Strangest Things* (cont.)

Tail Adaptations

Many reptiles use their tails as weapons or to fool the enemy. Some lizards have strong, stout tails that are covered with spines. When frightened, they scoot for their burrow and dive in headfirst, with their tail sticking out. If an enemy gets too close—smack with the tail spines! A small rubber boa has a round, blunt tail that resembles a boa's head. The small boa uses its tail to fool enemies by coiling up into a ball with its head at the bottom of the coil. As its tail curls out of the top, enemies unfortunately mistake it for the head and grab the wrong end. Some reptiles can drop their tail if the need arises. A lizard's tail is made up of several bones called **vertebrae**. These vertebrae have cracks where they can break off. When a lizard drops its tail, the tail continues to wiggle and gives the lizard an opportunity to escape. Don't worry, it can grow a new one by a process called **regeneration**.

Camouflage

Natural **camouflage**, or blending in with the surroundings, helps an animal to ambush prey or hide from enemies. Reptiles have developed different methods of camouflaging themselves. The European viper is the same color as sand. It flattens itself into the sand, making it difficult to see. The alligator snapping turtle looks like a stone if it lies motionless in water. It sits patiently waiting for prey to get close enough and then snatches it into its powerful jaws. Lizards are famous for their camouflage talents. They can alter their colors or patterns in a matter of seconds. Once their color matches their surroundings, it is very difficult for another animal to see them.

Bluffing

Bluffing the enemy is another behavior some reptiles use to avoid danger. They do this by acting bigger or more dangerous than they really are. They often scare their enemies away by pretending to be something they are not. A rat snake can act like a dangerous rattlesnake by

hissing and vibrating its tail. In dead leaves, the tail can make a sound that is similar to the rattle of a rattlesnake. The frilled lizard is only eight inches long. This lizard raises a colorful, frilled collar of skin around its neck, hisses loudly, puffs up its body with air, rises up on its clawed hind legs and waves its tail back and forth when it is frightened. This sudden ferocious movement that makes the lizard appear bigger and very dangerous is very effective at startling an enemy. Some snakes like to play dead to bluff the enemy; others have coloration similar to poisonous snakes and can fool the enemy into thinking they are something else. The horned lizard can squirt blood at enemies over seven feet away to catch the predator off-guard.

Reptile Behavior: *Reptiles Do the Strangest Things (cont.)*

Meeting a Mate—Courtship Behavior

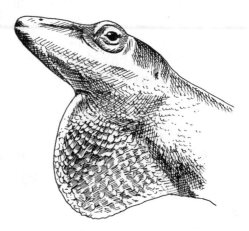

Like all animals, reptiles must create new members of their species, or they would eventually die out. The process by which a species creates members of its own kind is called **reproduction**. Reptiles require both a male and a female in order to mate. They mate only at certain times of the year. Some reptiles, like the green turtle, only mate every two or three years. Male lizards become very colorful when it's time to mate. Their coloration is how they attract a female. They also attract mates by making certain sounds. A male alligator roars to meet and attract a female. The male anole lizard can fan out the skin of its throat. During mating season, its fan is brightly colored and warns the other male lizards to stay away. The display also tells the female it is ready to mate. Rattlesnakes will compete for a mate with a special "dance." The two will twist and turn with their heads reared as they push and press against each other. It looks like a fight, but neither snake gets hurt.

Reptiles do not depend on water for reproduction as fish and amphibians do. They reproduce by internal fertilization. The eggs are fertilized inside the female's body. A developing young reptile, called an **embryo**, then grows within the egg. After mating, many reptiles lay their eggs in sand, soil, or on rotting logs. Some bury their eggs in nests deep in the ground, while others lay their eggs in depressions in the ground. The eggs are usually laid where they will keep warm, to ensure proper development. After they lay their eggs, most reptiles leave them. The young hatch and receive no parental care. An exception is the American alligator. A female alligator provides care for its eggs and young. It covers the eggs and guards the nest from predators. After the eggs hatch, the mother carries the hatchlings in her mouth to water. The young follow their mother several weeks before going off on their own. Another amazing reproductive behavior is that of the sea turtles. These turtles make an incredible journey. The turtles **migrate** (make a seasonal movement) for thousands of kilometers to lay their eggs on the same beaches where they were hatched.

Maintaining the Delicate Balance—Seasonal Behaviors

A reptile's body temperature depends on its surroundings. It needs heat from the sun to keep its body working properly. When the temperature gets too high, it cools down in the shade. Reptiles that sense the climate is getting too cool perform a behavior called **hibernation**. During hibernation, reptiles hide and rest for long periods of time without eating or moving. They live off the fat stored in their bodies until warm weather returns. Reptiles that live in areas that get too warm hide during the hot summer months. Summer hibernation is called **estivation**.

Reptile Behavior: *Reptiles Do the Strangest Things (cont.)*

Reptile Senses

Reptile Vision

Sight is the sense that is most commonly used among reptiles. Most reptiles have very keen eyesight, except for the snake. Burrowing animals seem to lose some of their sense of sight. Snakes are very nearsighted and don't see details. They do sense movement, though, and a snake will often go past motionless prey. The eye of a reptile works much like a camera. Light enters the eye through a lens. The **iris** (colored portion) controls the amount of light that enters the eye. Behind the eyeball is a coating called the **retina**. The retina is the eye's "film." When light falls on the retina, it registers an image. The optic nerve sends the image to the brain, where it is "developed" into a "picture." Most reptiles have two eyelids and can blink. This keeps the eyes clean. A membrane covers the eye and offers protection. Alligators use this membrane when they dive to see clearly underwater. Snakes do not have eyelids; they have a clear scale that covers the eye for protection. Most vertebrates have vision cells called rods and cones, which were named for their shapes. **Rods** are light-sensitive so an animal that is **nocturnal** (active at night) has many rods and lacks cones. **Cones** are the cells responsible for color vision. Most nocturnal animals lack color vision. Many reptiles, such as lizards and turtles, have large numbers of cones and do have color vision.

Reptile Hearing

Most reptiles have an ear opening where sound enters and travels inside their head to the inner ear. Reptiles do not have a visible outer ear. Many have an eardrum that is visible on the outside of the head. Sounds come from vibrations that travel in the form of energy waves through matter, such as water or air. An eardrum picks up the wave vibrations and sends the message along the auditory nerves to the brain where it is interpreted as sound.

Snakes do not have an ear opening, but they can detect noises. Sound travels on the ground to the snake's lower jaw. The vibrations are picked up by the jaw and pass through its skull into the inner ear. Some snakes do not rely on sound at all, but are so sensitive to temperature changes that they can feel heat coming from the body of a warm-blooded animal. They have special organs called "pits" between their eyes and nostrils. The pits detect the rise or drop in body temperature.

Reptile Smell and Taste

Many reptiles have a **Jacobson's organ** on the roof of their mouth. It is used for taste and smell. Snakes and lizards use it to find food. They flick their tongues quickly in and out of their mouths; the tongue catches scent particles from the air. By touching their tongues on the Jacobson's organ, they can detect prey or enemies. Some reptiles smell much the same way we do. The molecules in the air enter the nose, and the information travels to the brain where it is registered as smell.

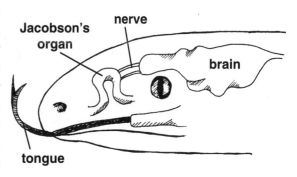

Reptile Behavior: *Reptiles Do the Strangest Things (cont.)*

How Reptiles Function

Reptiles take most of their body heat from their surroundings. Reptiles live in warm places; they depend on the heat from the sun to warm their bodies. A reptile's body needs to be warm so that its organs can work properly. They like it not too hot and not too cold. When their bodies get too warm, they estivate or move to cooler areas. When it gets too cold, they hibernate or bury themselves where the winter frost will not reach them. They live off the fat stored in their bodies until the weather warms again.

Reptiles have many ways of catching and eating food. They feed on a wide variety of things. Many reptiles are **carnivores**. Carnivores are animals that eat meat. They use their senses to track down prey, or sometimes they let their prey come to them. They hide quietly until an animal wanders by, and then they catch it. Most *chelonians* (reptiles in shells) and some lizards are **omnivores**. They eat both plants and meat. Snakes either constrict their prey by suffocating them or kill their prey with poison. Reptiles digest their food very slowly. They can go for long periods of time without needing to eat.

Name: _____ Date: _____

Reptile Behavior: *Reinforcement Activity*

To the student observer: Do you ever behave like these reptiles? _____

Analyze: Can you explain and give an example of a time you demonstrated a defensive, courtship, or metabolic (internal conditions) behavior?

_____

_____

Directions: Answer the following questions.

1. What are adaptations? _____

    _____

    _____

2. What is behavior? _____

    _____

3. What are the two forms of behavior? _____

    _____

4. Reptiles demonstrate mostly which form of behavior? _____

    _____

5. What are four methods that reptiles use for defense?

    a. _____

    b. _____

    c. _____

    d. _____

6. Give two examples of courtship behaviors used by reptiles.

    a. _____

    b. _____

7. What is an embryo? _____

    _____

8. What are two behaviors that reptiles use to maintain proper body temperature?

    a. _____

    b. _____

Name:_____ Date: _____

Scientific Investigation: *Student Lab*

Egg-Burying Behavior

To the student observer: How does burying the eggs benefit reptile reproduction? _____

_____

Analyze: Some reptiles bury their eggs under heaps of plant material and dirt or sand. The eggs remain there until they hatch. How do you think this behavior benefits the eggs?

_____

_____

Try this lab investigation and analyze your results.

Materials needed: Dirt
Dead plant material
Long thermometers

1. **Procedure:** Construct a compost heap outside your school by alternating layers of dirt and dead plant material. Build the heap until it measures 0.5 m (approximately 1.5 ft.) high. Using long thermometers, determine and record the temperature of the air and the temperature of the center of the compost heap. Record temperature measurements twice a week for four weeks.

Record Data:

Week	Air Temperatures		Compost Temperatures	
	#1	#2	#1	#2
# 1				
# 2				
# 3				
# 4				

Analyze results:

2. Graph the changes in air temperature over the four weeks. Do the same for the compost temperatures. How do they differ?

    _____

    _____

3. How do you think the temperature in the heap would benefit developing eggs? What would be some other advantages to burying the eggs?

    _____

    _____

Reptiles and Humans: *Keeping an Eye to the Future*

Today, many animals face a serious problem—their populations are declining. If an animal's numbers decline in population, we say the animal is threatened or endangered. **Endangered animals** are those in need of protection in order to survive. It's possible they could become **extinct** (no longer living). The animals that are already extinct are animals we will never see again. There are over 5,000 animals around the world that have been classified as endangered. There are two terms used for animals whose numbers are on the decline. Endangered animals are at immediate risk, while **threatened species** are at risk in the future. There are five main reasons animals find themselves on the road to endangerment: loss of **habitat** (home), **poaching** (unregulated hunting or illegal killing), overuse of pesticides or pollution of habitat, predators, and disease. Reptile populations are no exception; reptiles around the world face a greater risk now than ever before.

Reptiles and Humans

At one time, reptiles ruled the earth. Now, only four major groups of reptiles remain. The main concern lies in the destruction of their natural habitats. Some of the areas in which reptiles live are being lost at a frightening rate. The rain forests of the tropics and the shrub lands of Europe are two prime examples. Many reptiles have specially **adapted** (changed) to live in these areas. Governments have agreed to help some severely threatened species by protecting their habitats and passing laws prohibiting the exploitation of these animals for profit.

Many people are not sympathetic to the loss of reptile populations, letting their fears and ignorance of the role of the reptile in the natural world influence how they feel. Each living thing has a unique and irreplaceable beauty, as well as its own place in the balance of nature.

Humans and reptiles interact in a number of ways. Snakes, lizards, and turtles are commonly kept as pets. However, conservationists warn that people should not make pets out of reptiles that are rare in the wild. Over-hunting reptiles for their skins has led to the rapid decline of some species. Humans use the hides of reptiles to create articles of clothing, footwear, and other accessories. Reptiles that are farmed commercially can be used to provide food for people. It is not uncommon to see rattlesnake on a menu in the American Southwest. Alligator is used for local dishes in parts of Florida. Turtle soup is served in restaurants in the Caribbean and Asia; however, in many cases the turtles have been hunted illegally. Many farmers allow snakes to live in their barns to reduce the mice population. Some lizards eat harmful insects that destroy valuable crops. Researchers have studied venomous snakes and developed antivenin for snakebites and medicine for high blood pressure.

Reptiles play a helpful role in maintaining the delicate balance of nature. Most reptiles prefer to spend their days quietly searching for food, adjusting their body temperature, and avoiding danger. The increase of human population has been the greatest threat to reptiles and other animals that are facing endangerment. Fortunately, international laws prevent the sale and purchase of products made from the skins, bones, hides, or shells of endangered reptiles.

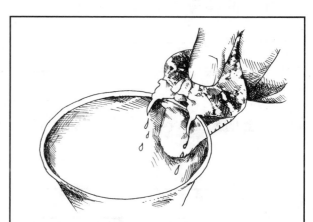

People sometimes "milk" the venom out of poisonous snakes and collect it to use in medicines. To milk a snake, a person holds it by the head and gently squeezes venom from the venom sac inside. The venom then drips out of the snake's fangs.

Name: _____ Date: _____

Reptiles and Humans: *Reinforcement Activity*

To the student observer: Why has it been difficult to get people to support efforts to save endangered reptiles?

_____

_____

_____

Directions: Complete the following questions.

1. What is a serious problem faced by many animals today? _____

   _____

   _____

2. What are the two terms used to describe a decrease in population?

   a. _____

   b. _____

3. Which term describes a more critical decrease in population? _____

   _____

4. What are two areas in which reptiles live that are disappearing at a frightening rate?

   _____

   _____

5. List three ways humans and reptiles interact.

   a. _____

   b. _____

   c. _____

6. List five main reasons animals travel the road to extinction.

   a. _____

   b. _____

   c. _____

   d. _____

   e. _____

Name: _____ Date: _____

Endangered Reptiles: *Research and Writing Project*

Analyze: What can you do to become a part of the solution for all endangered animals?

An Endangered Reptile: _____

1. Draw your reptile here and include why it is leaving its natural habitat or dying out; or draw it here and include what is being done to help it survive.

2. Where does the reptile live? _____

   _____

3. What does it look like? (color, size, special features) _____

   _____

4. What does it do? (a typical day, behaviors it has, etc.) _____

   _____

   _____

5. Why is it endangered? _____

   _____

   _____

6. Is anything being done to save this reptile? _____

   _____

* **Teacher Note:** Reproduce this form as a simple reporting device. Then have students attach their written report.

Name: _____ Date: _____

Endangered Reptiles: *How Can We Save Them?*

Which Reptiles Are At Risk?

Unfortunately, people have contributed to the thoughtless destruction of reptiles. Today, 35 North American reptiles are threatened with extinction. People have over-hunted and exploited reptiles for profit. We have caused severe pollution problems in their habitats. We have cleared forests, drained swamps, and developed coastal areas for housing and tourism. We realize now how important these reptiles are in the balance of nature. Today many people, groups, and organizations are trying to save them. Governments are passing laws to regulate the hunting of reptiles and the selling of these animals' skin, meat, shells, and eggs. Protected areas are being set aside solely for reptiles to use as a place to live and produce offspring. Let's hope these reptiles can survive and continue to be part of our complex biosphere.

Some Endangered Reptiles

Wood Turtles—*Clemmys insculpta*
   Range: USA; Nova Scotia to northern Virginia; Great Lakes Region
   Habitat: Woods, marshes, swamps
   Reason Endangered: Over-hunted

Batagur—*Batagur baska*
   Range: Southeast Asia
   Habitat: Tidal areas, estuaries
   Reasons Endangered: Excessive collecting of eggs; killing of adults for food

Spur-thighed Tortoise—*Testudo graeca*
   Range: North Africa; Southern Europe; Middle Asia
   Habitat: Meadows and woodlands
   Reason Endangered: Collected and exported as pets; many die due to unsuitable climate

Loggerheads—*Caretta caretta*
   Range: Temperate and tropical areas of the Pacific, Indian, and Atlantic Oceans
   Habitat: Coasts and open seas
   Reasons Endangered: Over-collecting of eggs; lack of hunting controls

Spectacled Caiman—*Caiman crocodilus*
   Range: Venezuela to southern Amazon basin
   Habitat: Slow, still waters, lakes, and swamps
   Reasons Endangered: Over-hunting; pet trade

Estuarine Crocodile—*Crocodylus porosus*
   Range: Southern India through Indonesia; southern Australia
   Habitat: Estuaries, coasts, and swamps
   Reason Endangered: Over-hunted for hide

Name: _____ Date: _____

Endangered Reptiles: *How Do We Save Them? (cont.)*

Green Turtle—*Chelonia mydas*
    Range: Worldwide
    Habitat: Coasts and open seas
    Reasons Endangered: Over-exploited for meat and eggs; disease from pollution

Galapagos Land Iguana—*Conolophus subcristatus*
    Range: Galapagos Islands
    Habitat: Arid land, coasts to volcanoes
    Reasons Endangered: Predators introduced into their area; over-hunted

Dumerils Boa—*Acrantophis dumerili*
    Range: Southwestern tip of Madagascar
    Habitat: Arid regions
    Reasons Endangered: Habitat loss; over-hunted for hide and pet trade

Reptile Research Project

1. Research to learn which reptiles need saving and add them to the list on these two pages.

_____

_____

_____

_____

_____

_____

_____

_____

_____

_____

_____

_____

_____

Name: _____ Date: _____

Research: *Reptiles Project*

To the student observer: Draw a card from your teacher's grab bag. The cards are equally divided between non-poisonous snakes, poisonous snakes, lizards, sea turtles, freshwater turtles, tortoises, crocodiles, and alligators, and there is a single tuatara card. Based on the luck of the draw, you must choose an appropriate species to research. Pick one that interests you. You will need to gather information about your reptile. Your research must include at least two resources. Follow your teacher's directions for the format and length of the presentation. Your project should include the topics listed below. Use this checklist to help you finish your project.

Topics: Completion of each topic is worth 10 points.

_____   I.   Description (What does your reptile look like?)

_____   II.   Drawing or photocopied picture (A visual aid)

_____   III.   Classification information (Use the chart discussed in class.)

_____   IV.   Size information (How big or how small is your reptile?)

_____   V.   Close relatives (What reptile is very similar to yours?)

_____   VI.   Location and diet (Where is your reptile found, and what is its diet?)

_____   VII.   Behavior (How does your reptile act, and why does it act that way?)

_____   VIII.   Life span (How long does your reptile usually live?)

_____   IX.   Reproduction (What is the usual number of offspring and gestation time?)

_____   X.   Conservation information and efforts

_____   *** Extra Effort:** Give two additional facts you learned during your research.

* Teacher Note: Place index cards labeled **non-poisonous snake**, **poisonous snake**, **lizard**, **sea turtle**, **tuatara** (only one), **freshwater turtle**, **tortoise**, **alligator**, and **crocodile** in a grab bag. Leave space for students to write their names and the specific reptile they will be researching on the cards. Use as many cards as needed for each student to get one.

     34

Name: _____ Date: _____

Research: *Reptiles Project (cont.)*

Reptile: _____

I.   Description: _____

_____

_____

_____

_____

_____

_____

II.   Drawing of your reptile:

_____

III.   Classification information:

Kingdom: _____

Phylum: _____

Class: _____

Order: _____

Family: _____

Genus: _____

Species: _____

Name: _____ Date: _____

Research: *Reptiles Project (cont.)*

IV. Size information: _____

_____

_____

V. Close relatives include: _____

_____

_____

VI. Location and diet:

Range: _____

Habitat: _____

Food: _____

VII. Behavior: _____

_____

_____

_____

VIII. Life span: _____

IX. Reproduction:

Number of offspring: _____

Gestation time: _____

X. Conservation information and efforts: _____

_____

_____

_____

* Extra effort: Two other interesting facts: _____

_____

_____

_____

_____

_____

Name: _____ Date: _____

Reptile Vocabulary: *Study Sheet*

To the student observer: This is a list of important terms used throughout the unit. Use this sheet to help you do the activities in the reptile unit. You can use this list of terms to help you study for the Unit Test.

1. **Amniotic Egg** - provides a complete environment for a developing embryo

2. **Brackish** - slightly salty water (fresh- and saltwater mixed)

3. **Camouflage** - the ability to blend in with surroundings

4. **Carnivore** - an animal that eats meat

5. **Dinosaur** - an early reptile, now extinct

6. **Diurnal** - active during the day

7. **Endangered** - animals with dangerously low numbers

8. **Estivation** - inactive state during the summer

9. **Estuary** - the mouth of a river; where the river meets the sea

10. **Fossil** - hardened remains or imprints in stone that provide an ancient record

11. **Herbivore** - an animal that eats plants

12. **Herpetology** - the study of reptiles and amphibians

13. **Hibernation** - inactive state during the winter

14. **Jacobson's Organ** - a sensory organ in snakes used to smell and taste

15. **Musk** - strong scent made by some reptiles

16. **Nocturnal** - active during the night

17. **Omnivore** - animal that eats both plants and other animals

18. **Paleontologist** - a scientist who studies fossils

19. **Pit Vipers** - poisonous snakes with sensory organs near their eyes

20. **Reptile** - a cold-blooded vertebrate with scaly skin

Name: _____ Date: _____

Reptiles: *Crossword Puzzle*

To the student observer: Show what you have learned by completing the puzzle below.

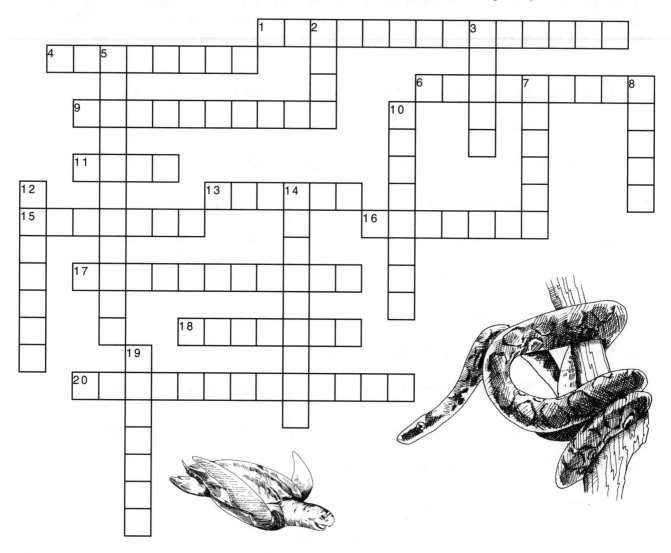

ACROSS
1. A _____ is a scientist who studies fossils.
4. _____ water is slightly salty.
6. _____ are now extinct.
9. Reptiles with low population numbers are _____.
11. The _____ feeds the embryo inside the egg.
13. A _____ can grow back its tail.
15. _____ animals are no longer living.
16. _____ are hardened remains or imprints in stone that provide an ancient record.
17. One of the major problems faced by animals that live on land is _____.
18. A _____ is called a "living fossil."
20. A scientist who studies reptiles and amphibians is called a _____.

DOWN
2. Reptiles lay eggs on _____.
3. Reptiles breathe with their _____.
5. One of the most important adaptations for life on land was the _____ _____.
7. Reptiles have thin, flat body coverings called _____.
8. A limbless reptile is called a _____.
10. A turtle that lives only on land is a _____.
12. A cold-blooded, scaly vertebrate is a _____.
14. An _____ is a member of the Crocodilian order.
19. *Reptilia* means "_____."

Name: _____   Date: _____

Reviewing Key Concepts: *Reptile Jeopardy*

Key Concepts:
- Reptiles are ectothermic (cold-blooded) vertebrates that have lungs, scaly skin, and a special type of egg.
- The age of the reptile was the Mesozoic Era.
- Early reptiles were successful because of their adaptations for life on land.
- There are four main groups of modern reptiles.

To the student observer: You may be familiar with a popular game show in which the answers are given and the contestants must try to provide the right questions. See if you can correctly complete the questions for each of the following answers.

1. **Answer:** The only two lizards in the world with venomous bites

   Question: What are _____?

2. **Answer:** A reptile that is considered to be the largest lizard

   Question: What is a (an) _____?

3. **Answer:** A young organism that hasn't fully developed yet, such as a snake in an egg.

   Question: What is a (an) _____?

4. **Answer:** Shelled reptiles

   Question: What are _____?

5. **Answer:** These cover the skin of reptiles to protect them and prevent water loss.

   Question: What are _____?

6. **Answer:** A special sensory organ in the mouth that receives scent particles from the air

   Question: What is a (an) _____?

7. **Answer:** Reptiles that do not have legs and are closely related to lizards

   Question: What are _____?

8. **Answer:** An animal whose body temperature is dependent on its surroundings

   Question: What is a (an) _____?

9. **Answer:** Organs a reptile uses to breathe

   Question: What are _____?

Name: _____ Date: _____

Reviewing Key Concepts: *Reptile Jeopardy (cont.)*

10. **Answer:** A large, aggressive, meat-eating reptile that lives in brackish water

    Question: What is a (an) _____?

11. **Answer:** A reptile that has become extinct

    Question: What is a (an) _____?

12. **Answer:** A substance produced in the glands of poisonous snakes

    Question: What is _____?

13. **Answer:** The ability of lizards to cast off a tail and then grow another one

    Question: What is _____?

14. **Answer:** A large snake that suffocates its prey

    Question: What is a (an) _____?

15. **Answer:** The oldest and smallest order of reptiles called "living fossils"

    Question: What are _____?

16. **Answer:** A reptile that makes an incredible journey to the same place it was hatched to lay its eggs

    Question: What is a (an) _____?

17. **Answer:** An evolutionary milestone that allowed vertebrates to reproduce on land

    Question: What is the _____?

18. **Answer:** A large group of ectothermic vertebrates that have lungs, scaly skin, and lay a special kind of egg on land

    Question: What is a (an) _____?

19. **Answer:** The method of fertilization that takes place in reptiles

    Question: What is _____?

20. **Answer:** A modern reptile group that includes chameleons, iguanas, and geckos

    Question: What are _____?

* **Teacher Note:** Use this activity to check students' understanding of reptiles. It may be used as a reinforcement worksheet, as an evaluation tool, or simply as a fun game.

40

Name: _____ Date: _____

Reptiles: *Unit Test*

I. **Multiple Choice:** Write the letter of the correct answer on the line to the left of the question.

_____ 1. The Age of the Reptile was the _____ era.
    a. Cotylosaurs   b. Permian   c. Carboniferous   d. Mesozoic

_____ 2. Unlike the eggs of amphibians, the eggs of reptiles _____.
    a. are fertilized internally   c. hatch into larva
    b. are fertilized externally   d. have no shells

_____ 3. Turtles breathe with their _____.
    a. gills   b. lungs   c. gill slits   d. skin

_____ 4. _____ are ectotherms with dry, scaly skin that lay amniotic eggs.
    a. Salamanders   b. Iguanas   c. Toads   d. None of these

_____ 5. Poisonous snakes have special glands that produce _____.
    a. food   b. musk   c. antivenin   d. venom

_____ 6. _____ is a reproductive behavior of crocodilians that is different from most reptiles.
    a. Laying unprotected eggs   c. Providing care for the young
    b. Males incubating the eggs   d. Burying the eggs

_____ 7. Reptiles _____.
    a. are both predator and prey   c. have many defensive behaviors
    b. all of these   d. have a three- or four-chambered heart

_____ 8. _____ is not an adaptation for reptiles to live on land.
    a. Hibernation   c. Internal fertilization
    b. Special eggs   d. Waterproof skin with scales

_____ 9. A (an) _____ is a reptile that has a long, slender snout and is aggressive.
    a. crocodile   b. alligator   c. lizard   d. snake

_____ 10. Reptiles _____ in the winter to avoid cold temperatures.
    a. estivate   b. migrate   c. incubate   d. hibernate

_____ 11. A developing reptile inside the egg is called a (an) _____
    a. hatchling   b. baby   c. embryo   d. reptilia

_____ 12. The ability to blend in with the surroundings is called _____.
    a. herpetology   b. estivate   c. invisible   d. camouflage

Name: _____ Date: _____

Reptiles: *Unit Test (cont.)*

_____ 13. A scientist who studies fossils is called a _____.

      a. taxonomist   b. biologist   c. paleontologist   d. herpetologist

_____ 14. Lizards can drop their tails and grow a new one by a process called _____.

      a. amnion   b. diffusion   c. regeneration   d. chlorion

_____ 15. A reptile from a long time ago that is now extinct is the _____.

      a. dinosaur   b. tuatara   c. fossil   d. dragon

_____ 16. _____ animals have critically low population numbers.

      a. Threatened   b. Extinct   c. Endangered   d. Estuary

II. **Matching:** Put the letter of the definition in the space next to the word it matches.

_____ 1. Musk   A. Sensory organ in snakes

_____ 2. Amniotic Egg   B. Ancient record of life

_____ 3. Herpetology   C. Poisonous snakes

_____ 4. Fossil   D. Scent produced by some reptiles

_____ 5. Jacobson's Organ   E. Hunts other animals for food

_____ 6. Pit Vipers   F. Complete environment for the embryo

_____ 7. Estivation   G. Thin body covering for reptiles

_____ 8. Scales   H. Study of reptiles and amphibians

_____ 9. Yolk   I. Inactive state during the summer

_____ 10. Predator   J. Food source for the embryo

III. List four characteristics of reptiles.

    1. _____

    2. _____

    3. _____

    4. _____

Answer Keys

What is a Reptile? Reinforcement Activity (page 3)
To the student observer: Reptiles make up a class of vertebrates that are well-adapted to life on land.
Analyze: "Living fossils" means that the tuataras group are relatives of the now-extinct dinosaurs.
I.
RELATIVES
DEHYDRATION
REPTILES
VERTEBRATES
SPECIES
COLD-BLOODED
ECTOTHERMIC
TUATARAS
II.
1. Eggs
2. yolk
3. creepers
4. lungs
5. Fossil
III.
1. The four groups of reptiles:
   a. Snakes and lizards
   b. Alligators and crocodiles
   c. Turtles and tortoises
   d. Tuataras
2. The four main characteristics of reptiles:
   a. Lay eggs with a protective shell on land
   b. Dry skin with protective scales or plates
   c. Have a three- or four-chambered heart
   d. Use lungs to breathe

Herpetology: Reinforcement Activity (page 5)
To the student observer: Herpetology is a branch of science that studies amphibians and reptiles.
Analyze: They studied live specimens and dissections of specimens and realized they are different internally and developmentally.
1. Scientists thought they were closely related.
2. Ectothermic animals are cold-blooded animals that obtain heat from outside sources. (Body temperature changes with surroundings.)
3. Endothermic animals are warm-blooded animals that have to maintain a constant body temperature. (Body temperature remains the same.)
4. They do not have to maintain a constant body temperature in order to survive. This allows them to go for periods of time without eating. Warm-blooded animals would die.
5. A resting state for cold-blooded animals to survive the cold

6. If an animal estivates, it means that it must find a cool spot and slow down all body functions; its body temperature is too high.
7. Metamorphosis is a change in development as a young amphibian grows into an adult. Reptiles do not go through this process.

Dinosaurs: Reinforcement Activity (page 7)
To the student observer: They became extinct. No one knows exactly what happened to them.
Analyze: They were better suited to the changes in the environment, and they could adapt.
1. Paleontologists are scientists who study fossils.
2. Their hip structure: bird-hipped or lizard-hipped
3. A fossil forms when an organism's remains are preserved, when the remains turn to stone, or when the imprint of the remains or tracks are left in stone.
4. The climate changed, and they couldn't survive.
5. There are no records to give us this information.
6. *Dinosaur* means "terrible lizard." It comes from Greek.

Reptile Reproduction: Reinforcement Activity (page 9)
To the student observer: It provides a complete environment for the embryo and allows animals to reproduce on land.
I.
1. The shelled egg protects the embryo and keeps it moist.
2. An amniotic egg has everything an embryo needs to finish developing. It has four special membranes for protection.
3. The yolk is the food supply.
4. The amnion membrane surrounds the floating embryo.
5. Oxygen enters through the pores in the shell.
6. Young reptiles are called hatchlings.
II. The parts of the reptile amniotic egg:
   a. shell   b. chorion
   c. yolk sac   d. yolk
   e. air space   f. embryo
   g. amnion   h. egg membrane
   i. allantois

Classification: Reinforcement Activity (page 11)
To the student observer: It makes identification and learning about the organism easier.
Analyze: They might appear similar to another organism on the outside, but upon looking inside, they may be more similar to a different organism.

1. Classifying means putting them into groups to make it easier to identify and learn about them.
2. Scientists classify organisms to organize and communicate information and to help identify new organisms.
3. A taxonomist is a scientist who studies the science of classifying organisms.
4. The classification of reptiles is based on their common ancestors.
5. The four main orders of reptiles are:
   a. Squamata: snakes and lizards
   b. Chelonians: turtles and tortoises
   c. Crocodilians: crocodiles and alligators
   d. Rhynchocephalia: tuataras
6. Five things scientists use to classify organisms:
   a. Physical features
   b. Cells
   c. Growth and development
   d. Blood
   e. Internal structures

Classification of Modern Reptiles: Reinforcement Activity (page 17)

Analyze: Accept all logical answers. Students should realize this could lead to an antivenin that could be used on all snake bites. We might find a chemical that people could keep in their first aid kits for snake bites.
1. Rhynchocephalia, the tuataras, has only a single species.
2. Turtles live in water and have thin, light shells. Tortoises live only on land and have thick, heavy shells that are dome-shaped.
3. The turtle's back and ribs are part of the shell.
4. An alligator has a short, broad, U-shaped snout, and a crocodile has a long, narrow, V-shaped snout with a visible tooth on either side.
5. Crocodilians are different because they have a four-chambered heart and they care for their young.
6. Lizards and snakes have a sense organ called the Jacobson's organ. The tongue picks up scent particles in the air.
7. Lizards break off their tails to escape from predators.
8. Snakes can unhinge or dislocate their jaws to swallow large prey.

Applying Main Ideas: Which Reptile Is That? (page 18)
1. Reptile identification:
   a. Turtle   b. Tuatara   c. Snake
   d. Lizard   e. Tortoise   f. Alligator
   g. Crocodile

Reptile Orders: Word Search (page 18)

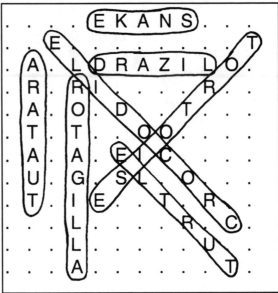

Reptile Orders: Reinforcement Activity (page 19)

To the student observer: Reptile Identification
1. Tuatara
2. Gopher tortoise, terrapin, leatherback
3. Gavial, alligator
4. Cottonmouth, chameleon, flying dragon, king snake, anaconda, boa, skink, iguana, cobra
5. Triceratops, stegosaurus

Snakes in Your Backyard: Research and Observation (page 20)

To the student observer: Answers will vary. Possible answers: swimming in a lake, walking in the timber, mowing the grass.

Teachers: Remember there are only four groups of poisonous snakes in the United States: rattlesnakes, copperheads, cottonmouths, and water moccasins. There are approximately 20 species. Every state but Maine, Alaska, and Hawaii has at least one venomous species.

Snakes: Fact or Fiction Reinforcement Activity (page 21)

1. Fact	9. Fiction
2. Fiction	10. Fact
3. Fiction	11. Fact
4. Fact	12. Fact
5. Fact	13. Fiction
6. Fiction	14. Fact
7. Fiction	15. Fact
8. Fact	

Reptile Behavior: Reinforcement Activity (page 27)
Analyze: Answers will vary.
1. Adaptations are traits that help reptiles survive in their habitats.
2. Behavior is the way an organism acts.
3. Behaviors can be innate or learned (acquired).
4. Reptiles demonstrate mostly innate forms of behavior.
5. Four methods reptiles use for defense are:
   a. Running and hiding
   b. Tail adaptations
   c. Camouflage
   d. Bluffing
6. Examples of courtship behavior are: lizards become brightly colored; rattlesnakes do a special dance; alligators roar to meet a mate.
7. An embryo is a developing reptile still inside the egg.
8. a. Hibernation
   b. Estivation

Scientific Investigation: Student Lab (page 28)
To the student observer: Eggs are easy prey, so burying them ensures that some will survive.
Analyze: Burying their eggs under heaps of plant material and dirt or sand helps keep the eggs at a proper temperature so the embryos can develop properly.
Record Data:
1. Answers will vary. Check students' readings closely.
Analyze Results:
2. Answers will vary. Readings should show greater differences in the air than in the compost pile.
3. Eggs need to maintain a constant temperature for proper embryo development. The temperatures shouldn't vary **as much** in the compost heap. The air temperature should vary greatly. Burying the eggs also hides them from predators.

Reptile and Humans: Reinforcement Activity (page 30)
To the student observer: They are not sympathetic to the loss of reptiles because they are afraid of them.
1. Their numbers are declining; they are becoming endangered or threatened.
2. a. endangered
   b. threatened
3. A more critical decrease in population is called endangered.
4. Two areas in which reptiles live that are disappearing at a frightening rate are rain forests and the shrub lands of Europe.
5. Any three:
   a. Humans keep them as pets.
   b. Humans farm reptiles for commercial profit. They use their hides for clothing, shoes, and accessories.

c. Humans study them for developing medications.
d. Farmers keep snakes to control mice populations.
6. a. Loss of habitat
   b. Over-hunting or poaching
   c. Predators
   d. Disease
   e. Pollution or overuse of pesticides

Reptiles: Crossword Puzzle (page 38)

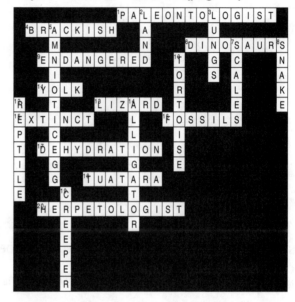

Reviewing Key Concepts: Reptile Jeopardy (pages 39–40)
1. Gila monsters and the Mexican beaded lizard
2. Komodo dragon
3. embryo
4. turtles and tortoises
5. scales
6. Jacobson's organ
7. snakes
8. cold-blooded animal or ectotherm
9. lungs
10. crocodile
11. dinosaur
12. venom
13. regeneration in lizards
14. constrictor
15. tuataras
16. sea turtle
17. amniotic egg
18. reptile
19. internal fertilization
20. lizards

45

Reptiles: Unit Test (pages 41–42)
I. Multiple Choice:

1. d	9. a
2. a	10. d
3. b	11. c
4. b	12. d
5. d	13. c
6. c	14. c
7. b	15. a
8. a	16. c

II. Matching:

1. D	6. C
2. F	7. I
3. H	8. G
4. B	9. J
5. A	10. E

III. The main characteristics of reptiles: (any four)
1. Lay eggs with a protective shell on land
2. Dry skin with protective scales or plates
3. Two pairs of legs with clawed feet
4. Use lungs to breathe
5. Have a three- or four-chambered heart
6. Are cold-blooded
7. Are vertebrates

Bibliography

Biggs, Daniel, and Ortleb. *Life Science.* Glencoe/McGraw-Hill, 1997.

Kalman, Bobbie. *What Is a Reptile?: The Science of Living Things.* Facts On File Publications, 1985.

McCarthy, Colin. *Reptile: Eyewitness Books.* Alfred A. Knopf, Inc., 1991.

Miller, Sara Swan. *Snakes and Lizards: What They Have in Common.* Franklin Watts, Grolier Publishing, 2000.

Miller, Sara Swan. *Turtles: Life in a Shell.* Franklin Watts, Grolier Publishing, 1999.

Pollock, Steve. *The Atlas of Endangered Animals.* Facts On File Publications, 1993.

Ricciuti, Edward. *Reptiles: Our Living World.* Blackbirch Press, Inc., 1993.

Strauss, Lisowski. *The Web of Life: Biology.* Scott Foresman-Addison Wesley, 2000.